who?

Jean-Henri Fabre
장 앙리 파브르

Biography Comic
who? ⑳ Jean—Henri Fabre

개정판 1쇄 인쇄 2014년 3월 5일
개정판 1쇄 발행 2014년 3월 10일

글 박연아
그림 크레파스
번역 자넷 재완 신
감수 김수희
펴낸이 김선식

책임편집 이유미 **디자인** 박효영
콘텐츠개발팀장 김선영 **콘텐츠개발팀** 박효영, 이유미, 김선민, 조서인
마케팅본부 이상혁

펴낸곳 스튜디오 다산 **출판등록** 2013년 11월 1일 제414-81-37694
주소 경기도 파주시 회동길 37-14 3층
전화 02-702-1724(기획편집) 02-703-1725(마케팅) 02-704-1724(경영관리)
팩스 02-703-2219 **who클럽** cafe.naver.com/dasankids
종이 월드페이퍼(주) │ **인쇄** (주)현문 │ **제본** 광성문화사

ISBN 979-11-5639-012-1 (14740)

who?
Jean-Henri Fabre
장 앙리 파브르

글 **박연아** | 그림 **크레파스** | 번역 **자넷 재완 신** | 감수 **김수희**

Dasan Kid

Jean-Henri Fabre

French entomologist, December 22, 1823 ~ October 11, 1915

Jean Henri Fabre is a scientist who wrote the best textbook on insects called *Souvenirs Entomologiques*. Henri grew up in a very poor family. His parents decided to raise ducks in order to earn a side income, but it was Henri who actually took care of them. While he was taking care of them, he becam familiar with all of the animals and insects in the woods.

Despite his poverty during childhood, Henri was quite diligent in his studies. Usually the poor had to labor from early morning until night just to make ends meet, leaving little opportunity for study. Henri enjoyed observing nature and discovering the secrets of different things. He pursued his studies and became a teacher, teaching poor children like himself the joy of learning.

While he taught at Ajaccio School on the island of Corsica, Fabre also began doing research on the island's plants, snails, and shells. He realized the joy of discovering something new and learning about it, and began researching insects on his own.

He would test the facts that were in the entomology books of his time and continue to observe and search for the answers to his own questions. Although poverty remained with Fabre, he continued to work as a teacher and do research.

Fabre wrote a paper about the facts he found through his observation and research. His work became recognized in the academic world and he received the highest honor given in France, the Legion d'Honneur Award.

His greatest accomplishment was the book he wrote called *Souvenirs Entomologiques*. Containing a lifetime of observation and research, *Souvenirs Entomologiques*, which Fabre spent 28 years writing, is still the most loved entomology book today.

장 앙리 파브르

프랑스의 곤충학자, 1823년 12월 22일 ~ 1915년 10월 11일

파브르는 최고의 곤충 이야기 『곤충기』를 남긴 과학자입니다. 파브르는 어릴 적 매우 가난한 집에서 생활했습니다. 부모님은 돈을 벌기 위해 오리를 키우기로 했는데, 오리를 보살피는 건 파브르였습니다. 파브르는 오리를 키우며 숲 속의 친구들과 친해지게 되었습니다.

파브르는 어린 시절 가난에 시달리면서도 공부를 게을리 하지 않았습니다. 가난한 사람들은 이른 아침부터 밤까지 죽도록 일해야 겨우 먹고 살 수 있었고 배움의 기회가 거의 없었습니다. 자연을 탐구하고 사물의 비밀을 밝히는 일을 하는 것이 더 즐거웠던 파브르는 공부하는 것을 포기하지 않고 교사가 되어 자신과 같은 가난한 아이들에게도 배움의 기쁨을 알게 해 주었습니다.

코르시카 섬의 아작시오 중학교에서 선생님으로 일하게 된 파브르는 교사로서의 일을 하며 동시에 코르시카 섬의 식물, 달팽이류, 조개류를 연구하기 시작했습니다. 새로운 것을 발견하고 그것을 연구하는 즐거움을 알게 된 파브르는 혼자서 곤충에 대한 연구를 시작합니다.

파브르는 당시 곤충을 다룬 책에 나온 내용을 실제로 실험하며 증명하거나 궁금증을 해소하기 위해 관찰과 연구를 계속했습니다. 가난은 평생 파브르를 따라다녔지만, 그는 교사로 일하는 동시에 연구를 계속해 나갔습니다.

파브르는 관찰과 실험을 통해 알게 된 사실을 논문으로 썼고 곧 학계에서 인정받는 성과를 이루었습니다. 그리고 프랑스 최고의 훈장인 레종 도뇌르 훈장을 받게 됩니다.

그의 업적 중 가장 큰 것은 곤충 이야기를 담은 책 『곤충기』입니다. 평생에 걸친 관찰과 연구를 바탕으로 28년 간 쓴 책 『곤충기』는 지금까지도 사랑받는 최고의 곤충 이야기입니다.

이 책을 만든 사람들

글 · 박연아

만화 스토리 작가로 활발하게 활동하고 있습니다. 순정 만화로 시작하여 학습 만화, 창작 만화, 동화까지 작업 범위를 넓혀 왔습니다. 현재는 인물의 어린 시절부터 성공에 이르는 과정을 통해 재미와 감동을 주는 인물 학습 만화 작업에 매진하고 있습니다. 작품으로는 학습 만화 『태극 천자문』(1권), 『제중원』, 『화랑세기와 미실』 등이 있습니다. (nicenoel@paran.com)

그림 · 크레파스

어린이들을 위해 새롭고, 재미있고, 즐거운 이야깃거리를 만드는 만화 창작 집단입니다. 세상을 바꾼 인물들의 삶을 통해 어린이들이 희망찬 미래를 만들어가길 바랍니다. 작품으로 『지식 똑똑 경제 리더십 탐구-긍정의 힘』, 『why? 서양 근대 사회의 시작』, 『why? 세계대전과 전후의 세계』 등이 있습니다.

번역 · 자넷 재완 신(Janet Jaywan Shin)

미국 메릴랜드 주에서 태어나고 자랐습니다. 메릴랜드 대학교에서 언어학을 전공하고 UCLA에서 응용언어학 석사 학위를 취득했습니다. 서울대학교 언어교육원에서 전임 강사, 서울대학교 사범대학교 영어교육과에서 초빙교수로 일했습니다. 감수한 책으로 『서울대생한테 비밀 영어과외받기』가 있고 고등학교 영어 교과서 교정 작업에 참여했습니다.

감수 · 김수희

연세대학교에서 역사를 전공했습니다. 이후 한국뿐 아니라 일본, 미국에서 한국어, 일본어, 영어를 가르쳐 왔으며 부모를 위한 영어교육용 책을 썼습니다. 영어교육채널 EBSe '엄마표 영어특강'에서 강의를 하며 홈스쿨, 알파벳과 파닉스, 다차원 테마 영어 수업 기법을 알리고 있습니다. 전국 각지에서 어린이 영어 교육에 대한 강연을 하며 창의적이고 열정적인 교수 법으로 영어를 배우고자 하는 어린이와 부모들에게 많은 도움을 주고 있습니다.

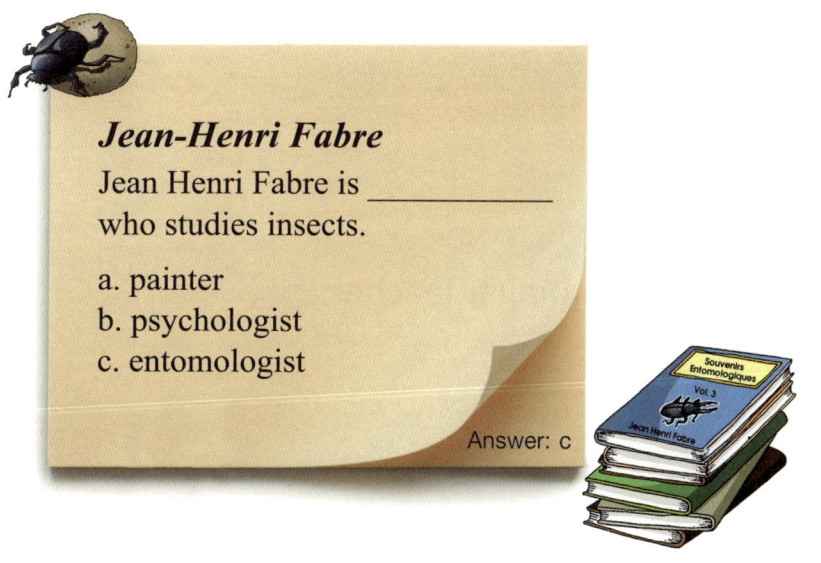

Jean-Henri Fabre

Jean Henri Fabre is _____ who studies insects.

a. painter
b. psychologist
c. entomologist

Answer: c

Contents

01 Son of a Poor Farmer

 Track 01 ▶

Jean-Henri Fabre was born in the winter of 1823, in a small Saint Leons village in southern France. He was called Henri when he was young.

Look, a very healthy baby boy.

We'll call you Henri.

Jean Henri Fabre! Haha.

The family's financial situation became more difficult after the birth of Henri's younger brother, Frederic.

Henri, you wanna come with me to Grandfather's house?

Grand-father's house?

Yes. You can eat all the potatoes you want and play with your uncle.

I wanna go!

Henri, you be a good boy.

Yes, Mama! Bye-bye, Frederic!

12

It's Grandfather's house!

CLOP CLOP

Welcome, Henri!

Hi, Henri! I'm your uncle.

Henri, how you've grown!

Hello, Uncle, Grandmother.

That night, Henri and his father had a delicious dinner at his grandfather's house.

The next day, Henri stayed at his grandfather's while his father went on home.

Wow! I've never seen a sausage this big before!

Hahaha! Bon appetit!

Take good care of Henri, Father.

Don't worry. Be safe.

At his grandfather's house, Henri had many animals to play with.

Hahaha, bet you can't catch me!

ARF ARF

Henri! Don't go too far!

Henri played all over the farm during the day, and listened to his grandmother's stories of old as she knitted at night.

The brave boy who chased away the monster became the hero of the village.

Wow! That's great!

Now, it's time for brave boys to get some sleep.

Goodnight, Grandma!

What should I play with tomorrow?

14

Of all the things he did, he got most excited about going with his grandfather into the woods to observe the insects and plants.

Henri, let's go meet some insects today.

Okay!

Toto, come with us!

WOOF WOOF

Alright, shall we see what kind of insects live in the woods?

Wow!

Henri, why don't you greet the insects?

Okay!

This is a cabbage white butterfly.

Oh!

During his time with his grandfather, Henri began to develop an interest in and love for nature.

Eventually, it came time for Henri to begin going to school. One day, his father came to take him back home.

Henri, Father's here!

Grandma, can't I stay here? I want to stay here longer.

I'm afraid there's no school here for you to attend.

...

No. I don't want go to school!

My good boy, Henri. Go to school and learn a lot from your teacher.

Waah! I don't wanna go to school!

I wanna live here! Waah!

The horse carriage Henri rode passed through snowy mountain paths...

...through streams...

...and finally to their Saint Leons home.

CLOP CLOP

18

Henri, my son!

You've gotten so big I can hardly recognize you.

Mother!

Frederic, say hello. It's your big brother.

Hello.

Heh heh, hello! I'm your brother, Henri.

It's so great to be all together!

Let's go inside, Henri. Dinner's ready.

Let's go, Frederic!

19

The next day after he returned to his home, Henri began to attend school.

Henri, say hello. This is your new teacher, Pierre Ricard.

Nice to meet you, Henri.

The classroom environment was rather bare at the time.

This is where you'll be studying. Go ahead and have a seat, Henri.

This is school? It looks boring.

20

Henri eventually became bored of studying at school.

Hmm, I wonder how the animals on the farm are doing. And the bugs in the forest, too.

It's a little stuffy, so let's open the door just a little.

Heh heh. Pigs!

Henri, who was bored in class, would sometimes pull mischievous pranks.

What are pigs doing here? Get out! Out!

Hahaha!

OINK OINK OINK

Thanks to the pigs we don't have to have class!

As time passed, Henri became more disinterested in school.

I'm home.

How was school, Henri? Did you have fun?

Yes, Mother.

One day, Henri's father gave him an animal picture book as a present. From that day on, animal picture books were a part of Henri's life and played a very important role in his life.

This is a present for you, to celebrate your starting school.

Wow, what is it?

Do you know what this is, Henri?

donkey

Donkey.

Right, donkey begins with 'd.'

Henri learned how to read and write as he studied the picture book his father gave him.

Oh, this is how you write 'hippo.' And this is 'ostrich'!

It's easy to learn how to write the animals' names by seeing the name with the picture of the animal!

Hippo, hippo.

It looks like the hippo is yawning. Hahaha, this is fun.

Hey, I saw him in my book. Hello, squirrel!

With the help of his animal picture book, Henri began to have more interest in his school studies.

02 Befriending Nature

I think we need more money if we want to give the kids a better education.

Just feeding them is starting to stretch our budget.

So I was thinking, what if we raise ducks?

Ducks?

Ducks are easy to raise. If we raise them by the nearby stream, it won't require any extra money.

I heard that we can feed them the beef tallow left over from making candles which will fatten them up. And our neighbor who makes candles will give us the tallow leftovers for cheap.

That sounds great. Let's raise some ducks!

What is this, Father?

We have to keep them warm until they hatch.

They're duck eggs.

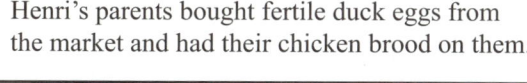

Henri's parents bought fertile duck eggs from the market and had their chicken brood on them.

Take good care of the duck eggs.

CLUCK CLUCK

Hahaha!

26

Two weeks passed and the ducklings grew quite a bit.

This place is too small now for you guys.

I'd better take the ducks to the stream.

Henri guided the ducks to the stream down the hill.

QUACK
QUACK

If we go a little bit further, you'll be able to swim and find lots of things to eat. Everyone, follow me!

We're here!

 **Track 11** ▶

Henri passed a pond that frequently dried up from being used by all the villagers. He took the ducks to a wide stream that was over the hill.

Wow! Nobody's here! I'm glad we came here.

Alright, swim all you want!

QUACK QUACK

The stream was like heaven to the ducks.

Hahaha!

30

Now it's time for me to play, too.

Whenever Henri became curious about something, he would observe it carefully.

What's this?

And if he had a question, he would investigate it until he found the answer. Henri's observation skills would become the foundation for him to later become an entomologist.

Wow, these must be tadpoles!

Whoa, what's this?

I'd better go home and find out more about this golden insect! Heh heh.

Henri was so busy exploring the nearby woods that he didn't realize the time passing by.

Wow, crystals!

They look kinda like shells and also like goat horns. How is it that these are inside rocks? Let's take them home.

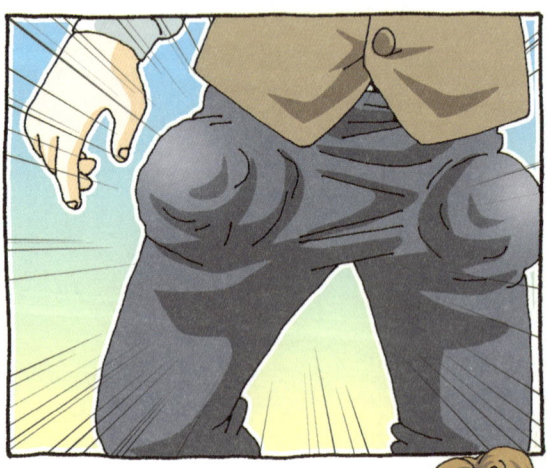

I guess I'd better head home.

Alright, time to go home now.

That's enough for today. Let's come back tomorrow!

Henri, your pockets are ripping! You can at least feed grass to the rabbits, but those rocks can't be used for anything. And they're ripping your pants. You don't have enough clothes as it is.

I just thought the rocks were neat...

Oh my! What are you doing with those bugs?

You've wasted your time away. Throw those out right now!

Henri's parents, who were weary of living a poor life, could not understand his interest in insects at all.

I just wanted to observe them up close. See you later, nameless bug!

BUZZZ

BUZZZ

34

Later, Henri's parents opened a restaurant in the prosperous city of Rodez.

Henri, look at our new restaurant.

Sigh. I guess I can't see my forest friends anymore.

Henri, don't worry. Things will get better.

Yes, Mother.

Tomorrow, let's find out about the school that you'll attend here.

Yes, Father.

Ten-year-old Henri entered a junior high school called the Royal College of Rodez.

We made an agreement that if you sing in the school choir, you can attend the school for free.

You can do it, can't you?

Yes.

I have to do this because of our family's situation. I can just play after choir practice.

Henri didn't like singing in the choir.

But when classes were finished, he was happy that he could go to a nearby field and look at the animals and insects there.

36

Henri spent much of his time reading. He was content to meet insects and animals like the honey bee, cicada, pigeon, crow, and goat inside of books.

I miss the woods by Grandfather's house so much. I wish I could go back to that time.

However, the Fabre family's financial situation continued to grow worse.
They had moved to Montpellier, but their business did not do well there, either.
In the end, they had to separate from each other and live in different places.

Every time we've started a new business, it hasn't done well so we've accumulated a lot of debt.

So we decided that your father and I will go to a bigger city to earn money.

And Frederic will stay at a relative's house.

For now, you need to live on your own. Do you think you can do it?

I'm fifteen now. Don't worry, Father.

Father, Mother, take good care of yourselves! Frederic, see you again soon!

Henri!

Take care, Henri!

CLOP CLOP

In 1838, the year he turned fifteen, Henri had to separate from his family and live on his own.

From now on, I've got to make my own money!

Alright, let's look for a job.

Avignon Teachers College

Henri sold lemons at the market during the day,
and worked at a construction site in the evenings.

Good work, Henri.
Here's today's wages.

Thank you.

It's not a lot, but
it's plenty for
me to get by
on my own!

See you
tomorrow!
Goodbye!

Take care!

See you
tomorrow,
Henri!

Track 17 ▶

Henri loved literature. One day, he found a collection of poems that he liked at the bookstore, and was in a dilemma.

Ah, that book!

Henri had just enough money to buy one meal. In order for Henri to buy the book he wanted, he would have to skip dinner.

It's the book of poems I've been waiting for. If I buy it, I'm not going to have any money left over. What should I do?

Okay. I'll skip tonight's dinner and buy the book!

I usually don't have enough to eat to make me full anyway. I'm better off buying the book! I might not be able to buy it later when it's all sold out.

He did not have money for a place to stay either, so he would spend nights at a park or under a bridge. The moon would be his light with which he would read his book of poems.

I'll stay here for tonight!

For Henri who couldn't complete his schooling because of money, reading was a huge joy for him. It was with this kind of effort that he would later be able to write *Souvenirs Entomologiques*.

Yawn, is it already morning? I'd better go to work now.

Accepting new students at Teachers College?

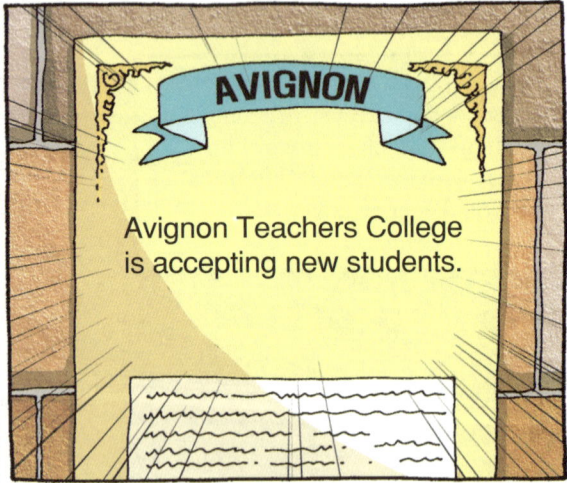

Avignon Teachers College is accepting new students.

If I can pass the exam, I can go to school for free and live in the dormitory. This is a great opportunity!

He's working hard out here and studying at the same time. What a good kid.

There's one thing everyone knows about Henri, and that's that he's diligent.

Despite his difficult circumstances, Henri's desire to learn something new and gain knowledge was greater than his desire to make a living. Consequently, he applied for admission to Avignon Teachers College.

Alright! I can do it!

Henri, who had studied whenever he had some time on the job, took the exam to apply for the school.

I wonder where my name is.

1 Jean-Henri Fabre

2 Pa

3

Jean-Henri Fabre!

Hahaha! I passed! And with the highest score at that!

Henri passed the Avignon Teachers College entrance exam with the highest score.

He must've gotten the highest score.

Wow, first place. That's pretty good.

In 1839, Henri turned sixteen.

Mother, Father, I'll be able to join you very soon!

Contrary to Henri's expectations, unfortunately, classes were repetitive and boring.

Today, we'll do a dictation on the sentences we learned yesterday.

I would rather study something else... When will I get the chance?

Why do bees have a stinger? Is it to protect themselves from danger?

Ow!

Jean Henri Fabre!

If you keep fooling around in class, you will get a zero on your next exam!

If you want to continue studying here, you'd best pay attention in class!

Ah, I let my mind wander again...

I'm sorry, sir.

Alright, there's not much time before the next exam. Open your books.

If I don't want to fail, I'd better study hard.

48

He had the highest score on the entrance exam, but he did not do well on the first exam.

Gasp, I almost failed the exam.

Report Card
Jean Henri Fabre

Lazy student of average intelligence. Average student.

I'm going to study hard from now on to finish the teachers college coursework in two years! Then with the extra year left over, I should be able to study whatever I want.

Henri studied hard just as he had determined to do. He was able to finish the teachers college coursework in two years.

Congratulations on passing the graduation exam, after completing the coursework in two years.

Thank you, dean.

It usually takes three years to complete the coursework. In the final year, you can stay here at school and study whatever you like.

Thank you, dean!

Henri completed the teachers college three-year curriculum in two years, and stayed on to continue studying. He studied languages by reading books in Latin and Greek.

In order to write well, you have to know many languages.

Then one day, Henri had an eye-opening experience. It was the first day of chemistry class. The natural science teacher began an experiment to produce oxygen.

We will see if oxygen is produced from manganese dioxide when we use sulfuric acid. Watch carefully and follow along.

It looks dangerous. Will oxygen really be produced?

Aaah!

Ack! It went in my eye!

Let's first go wash your eye out.

Ugh!

The chemistry experiment they were anticipating was a flop and there was no time to do the experiment properly before class ended.

Clean it out well and you'll be okay.

Ah, I think it's better now. Thanks for your help.

It's good you didn't get hurt any worse than you did.

We didn't get to complete the experiment but it was a good experience.

If I were the teacher, I would have observed the students first before starting the experiment. This accident happened because the teacher was not paying attention to the students.

Education is not a one-way street where knowledge is simply passed down.

The important thing is to draw out the students' potential. A good teacher is one who can do that.

If the teacher had paid more attention to the students, this kind of accident could have been prevented.

Alright, I've decided. I'm going to teach! I'm not going to stop at learning for myself. I'm going to find students' hidden potential and lead them. I'm going to be a teacher who experiments and works together with the students, and keeps on learning!

If I want to be a teacher and teach children, I've got to study more.

Once he determined that becoming a teacher would be his objective, he studied even harder.

He kept digging through the books until he found answers to the things he didn't know.

In order to become a good teacher, he read and studied many more books than he had in the past.

Because he studied so hard, Henri graduated with top grades.

Congratulations, Jean-Henri Fabre.

Thank you.

In 1842, Henri was appointed as a teacher at Carpentras School, which comprised of both an elementary and junior high school.

I'm glad to meet you all today. My name is Jean-Henri Fabre, and I will be your teacher.

Becoming a Teacher

04

At the time, education in France was not highly valued and teachers were not well-respected. A teacher's salary was very low, so Henri would earn just enough to buy some chickpeas and a little wine each month.

Although his salary was barely enough for necessities, Henri worked hard at teaching his students.

Today we will do an experiment in which we create oxygen. Is everyone ready?

How in the world is this relevant to us? It's boring and takes away from the time we can be working.

Sulfuric acid is dangerous, so be very careful when you're handling it. When I was a student, a distiller shattered and the sulfuric acid flew out and burned one of my friends.

When class is over, I've got to go straight to the farm to help out...

I don't know why we have to do these useless experiments.

Alright, you combine manganese dioxide and sulfuric acid like this.

I was just as poor as these students, but I now realize the joy of learning and discovering something new.

I want to help these students develop a passion for learning, too.

Now, can you see it starting to boil?

Wow, it's bubbling!

Bubbles are forming, aren't they? Gas is being produced.

Something's appeared!

Shall we see what happens if we put a flame into a bottle that's filled with oxygen?

The flame that was dying is now blazing higher, isn't it? This is proof that oxygen was produced!

Wow!

That's neat!

It's easy to understand and remember things that have been demonstrated through experiments.

If there were no oxygen, we wouldn't be able to breathe, right? Oxygen is a gas that is essential for us to live.

If there were no oxygen, animals and plants wouldn't be able to live. Oxygen is one of the most abundant elements on the face of the earth. It is one of the elements that make up the Earth's surface and the sea.

There is a lot of science like this hidden in nature.

It is a fascinating and admirable task to be able to observe and learn from experiments.

This time, let's have class outside so that we can learn about various plants and insects.

Our other teachers never let us have class outside.

Yeah, Mr. Fabre is different.

Henri unlike other teachers, often took the students outside to observe insects and animals. The students began to gradually love learning new things in Henri's class.

Having class outside is fun.

Class is getting a lot more interesting.

Look at this, Mr. Fabre! It's a grasshopper!

Shall we learn a little about grasshoppers?

There are many varieties of grasshoppers and insects. The rice grasshopper, the band-winged grasshopper, the oriental long-headed grasshopper, and the migrating locust all belong to this category.

Ewww, gross!

The grasshoppers like to mate when the weather is dry like today. That's why we can see a lot of them.

My father's a farmer and he hates grasshoppers!

That's because grasshoppers damage the crops.

The grasshoppers have a huge appetite and can eat a whole field of grain.

But you don't have to worry too much because there are insects and animals that eat grasshoppers, such as spiders, praying mantises, and frogs.

I didn't know that creepy spiders were a beneficial insect.

Isn't learning fun when you can see and feel for yourself like this?

Yes, Mr. Fabre!

The students began to really like Henri's teaching methods. And Henri did his best to teach the students well.

Okay. Your homework will be to read a book about insects and be ready to share about it with the class.

Yes, sir!

As word spread about Henri's class, more students began to apply to the school where he was teaching.

I want to take Mr. Fabre's class!

I want to attend this school, too!

Kids, what are you doing there?

Mr. Fabre, we're observing a beehive.

Ah, the bee is transporting honey to the hive!

Sir, can we try tasting it?

BZZZZZ

Sure. It's very sweet honey.

It looks like this mason bee is living on its own.

I thought bees lived in big colonies but I guess that's not always true.

If I record what the students and I observe, it will make good teaching material.

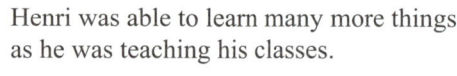

Henri was able to learn many more things as he was teaching his classes.

Here's more information about the mason bee.

We were right about the mason bee living on its own. What an interesting bee.

After Fabre read books about the mason bee, he spent his entire month's wages to buy *Natural History of the Articulata*. In the course of his reading this book over 100 times, he decided that he wanted to write a book himself.

Hmm, I'd like to write a story like this.

Mr. Fabre wrote this book!

Wow, look at this insect! It's really fascinating!

I hope that children can read my book and learn about insects and realize the value of nature!

I'm not satisfied with this book. If I can rewrite this in a more lively way, it could be a really interesting book.

I definitely want to write a book like that some day!

We can call the observation of insects living in nature and the recording of these observations a true academic study of insects.

It was at this time that Henri decided that he wanted to write his own special stories about insects.

In 1844, 21-year-old Henri married a fellow teacher at the school where he was teaching, Marie-Cesarine Villard.

WAAH WAAH

As his family size began to increase, Henri's finances became tighter.

It's hard to even buy one book on an elementary teacher's salary. I need to study more and become a high school teacher.

If you do that, you'll probably have more time to do research.

Even though money was tight, Henri would buy experiment equipment for his students with his own money.

It'd be nice if the school had funds for this, but for now, this should be enough to conduct basic experiments.

Because he spent his already small salary on teaching supplies, he was always short on living expenses.

My pay is so meager. it's hard to get by.

Hmm. If I had a larger salary, I could conduct so many more experiments with the students and prepare better for my classes...

But there were times when he wouldn't get paid for months at a time.

This is our last loaf of bread, honey.

I don't know what we're going to do.

I haven't gotten paid in months.

There isn't enough bread to go around. It's hard to buy even if we have enough money because of the high demand for it.

I'd better study more and become a college professor. Then, I'll have more time to research.

You can do it, dear. I know you can.

Today I'll finish the insect story that I started to tell you yesterday.

Which insect is it about?

Mr. Fabre, we wanna hear!

Guess which one it is! This insect has a stinger.

A bee!

A beetle!

What else do you think an insect with a stinger has?

I know!

I know!

When I see students who previously had no interest in class whatsoever become so excited about class, it makes me glad I became a teacher.

69

In order to become a high school teacher, Henri took on university studies.

Henri passed the baccalaureat exam, which he needed to enter university, and took the mathematics and physics teachers' licensing exam.

Henri finally received the teacher's license that he really wanted.

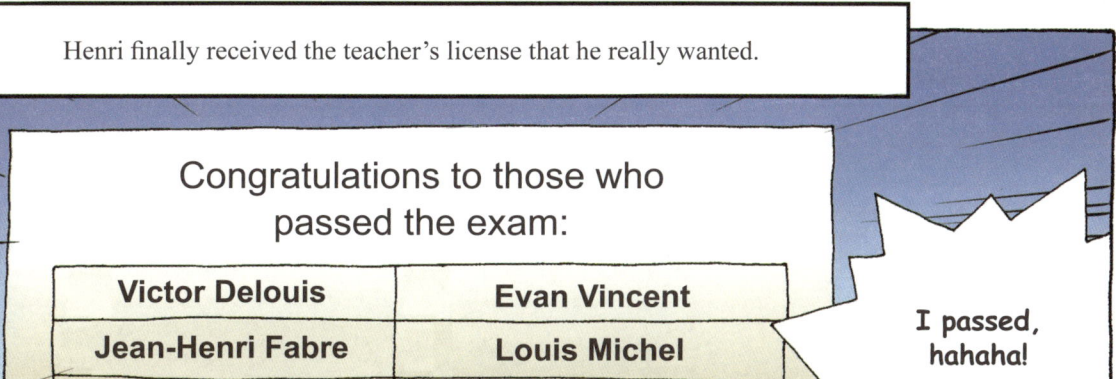

Congratulations to those who passed the exam:

Victor Delouis	Evan Vincent
Jean-Henri Fabre	Louis Michel
Frederic Simon	Gil Fournier

I passed, hahaha!

Honey, I passed!

Congratulations, dear! That's so great!

You worked so hard.

You worked even harder. Now we don't have to worry anymore.

Henri ended up going to Corsica Island to be a physics teacher at Ajaccio Junior High School.

05 Encounters on Corsica Island

Corsica Island was a completely new place to Henri. He decided that he would study all of the different types of snails and hellfish here.

Wow, the color of this shell is quite unusual.

The pattern on this one is amazing!

Around that time, Esprit Requien, a famous biologist came to Corsica Island to do research.

Huh? Who is that? He looks new...

What is he looking at?

Hello. I'm Jean Henri Fabre. I don't think I've seen you around before.

Nice to meet you, Mr. Fabre.

I'm Esprit Requien. I've come here to study the plant life on the island.

Aren't you the famous biologist, Dr. Requien?

I don't know about famous, but I am a biologist.

It's an honor to meet you, sir.

Requien and Henri quickly became friends, and Henri came to work together with him.

This is my research lab.

Nice to meet you.

Welcome, Mr. Fabre. We're Dr. Requien's lab assistants.

Corsica Island has many interesting things here so it's a great place for researchers. These are plants that I've collected and dried.

Ah!

There is a large variety of plants here.

76

I heard that you have been studying the plants of Corsica Island for a long time.

There is no other place that is as full of plant life as Corsica.

I would like to work together with you in your research!

Fabre, you are already my partner.

Work together with us to learn more about the plant life of this island!

Thank you, sir!

However, not long after, Esprit Requien passed away suddenly, leaving Henri devastated.

...

I can't believe I won't see him sitting here doing his research anymore...

I'm going to investigate the plants on the north side of the island. Come with me!

Look at this! This is the most beautiful plant I have ever seen!

Hahaha!

Dr. Requien!

78

Some time later, Professor Moquin-Tandon came to Corsica Island to continue Requien's work.

Welcome, Professor Tandon.

Nice to meet you.

The hotel is all booked. You can stay with us in our home, Professor.

Come with us.

Thank you, Mrs. Fabre.

Professor Tandon stayed at Henri's house. He came to Corsica to complete Requien's work of collecting plants to make a specimen collection.

Moquin-Tandon and Henri went around Mount Renoso collecting plant specimens.

Collecting plant specimens is important, but recording things accurately is extremely important.

When you record your observations about a plant, try to write sentences with some personality.

Sentences with personality!

You must always have an open mind. If your thinking has limits, then that's how much you won't be able to see.

I'll be sure to remember your advice.

One day, Tandon gave Henri a special lesson.

Mr. Fabre, you're studying snails these days, aren't you?

It's a great thing to do research, but when you do research, you have to find joy in the thing you are researching.

If there is no joy, you will quickly become weary of the work and when the results don't turn out well, you will easily give up.

Is he talking about the joy of discovering something new and learning about it?

You can dissect a snail with two needles.

The snail you previously knew can be rediscovered in a new way.

Fabre, from what I have observed of you, you seem better suited studying animals rather than plants.

Isn't that what brings you the most joy and satisfaction?

...

Right. While I've been on the island, I've wanted to learn more about the animals.

I'm much more excited about researching animals than about gathering plants! Alright, from now on, I'm going to focus on studying animals!

What you're trying to say is that you think I should work more with animals, right?

That's right.

Dissection will help you find out in more detail the structure of animals, and it will soon be the foundation of research.

That's it! Professor Tandon is reminding me of what I've always dreamed of doing.

I'm going to become a true researcher of nature as I continue to study the shellfish of this island.

Professor Tandon, thank you so much!

Just as he had learned from Professor Tandon, Henri collected and observed the shellfish of the island, and then dissected and studied them further.

The shape of this shell is different from the one I was just looking at! It must be a different species.

Oh, wow! I'm sure this shell is unique to Corsica.

Why do I suddenly feel so dizzy?

Everything feels like it's spinning...

Ahh!

Not long after he became a physics teacher, Henri fell ill with malaria.

His fever is so high... what should we do, doctor?

We have to be careful because if it's malaria, the fever will continue to rise. And it's also contagious.

Then, what should we do?

It's hard to treat here. I recommend you go to a bigger city.

Yes, doctor.

However, with his teacher's salary cut in half and finances tight, it was not easy to go to the city.

Dear, hang in there.

Eventually, Henri left the island to get treated by a doctor in the city.

How is he, doctor?

The fever has gone considerably. He should be alright.

What a relief!

...

Thank you, honey. It's because you took good care of me.

After he received medical treatment and recovered from malaria, Henri was offered the opportunity he had always wanted, to become a high school teacher. One day, the education department contacted him and invited him to teach at Avignon High School.

It's a letter inviting me to be a teacher at Avignon High School!

You are invited to be a teacher at Avignon National High School.

My name is Jean Henri Fabre and you will be studying together with me this year.

Henri diligently taught the students at Avignon High School.

Dear, you should get some rest.

My dream is to give lectures about animals and plants from a professor's platform. In order to do that, I have to get a math and physics degree as well as a masters in natural science.

After leaving Corsica, Henri's family had to live at Clara Sisters Abbey because of their financial situation. However, Henri did his best in the midst of these circumstances. He immersed himself in his natural science graduate studies in order to fulfill his dream of teaching about animals and plants.

While the rest of his family slept, Henri continued his studies by reading by the light of the stove.

Henri was reading a book about wasps, written by Leon Dufour who was known as the father of entomology.

This book stands out from the standard book that categorizes insects which have been collected and examined. It's amazing!

The descriptions of the insects are so detailed! This is the first book with such detailed descriptions of the structure and characteristics of insects.

Wait, this is the wasp.

Dufour says that the venom of the wasp acts as a preservative so that its food won't rot. Is that really so?

Alright, let's test it out tomorrow!

The next day, Henri set out to observe a wasp of the same variety as the wasp which Dufour had observed.

This is a good time to find wasps since they are best seen during the months of August and September.

Huh? This clearly sounds like a bee.

BZZZ

Aha! Over there!

I found one! It's a wasp!

BZZZ

Is it flying to its home?

This apparently is its home.

It's caught a jewel beetle.

I've gotta see now whether the wasp will sting the beetle with its venom and kill it, like Dufour had written!

The fact that it's excrementing is proof that it's not dead!

Let's try dropping a few drops of gasoline!

Oh, it's alive! Just as I expected!

Ten days later, in the same place...

Ten days have passed and it's still alive!

Touching it with a voltaic current made it flinch! This is proof that the jewel beetle is alive!

Shall we try giving it a voltaic current*?

The wasp didn't kill the jewel beetle with its venom! It only paralyzed it!

*votaic current: The first current created from a battery consisting of zinc and copper submerged in a sulfuric acid solution.

It paralyzes the beetle so that later when the bee's larva hatches, it can have something fresh to eat!

Incredible! Dufour's observations were false!

Up to now, research on insects has meant collecting, classifying, and dissecting them.

But there's so much that is unknown about the behavior and lifestyle of insects!

This is an entirely new field! There needs to be research where this area can be observed and recorded. I'm going to do it starting now!

06 Receiving the Legion d'Honneur Award

CD Track 44 ▶

Henri became fully concentrated on insect research.

Hmm, how do bees paralyze other insects?

Alright. Let's conduct an experiment.

We'll put some ammonia on the tip of a needle and prick it.

Ammonia

It can't use its arms and legs after being poked with a needle dipped in ammonia.

But not all beetles' nervous system will be affected by the toxin of a bee.

Then which beetles are suitable for the bees to sting?

Not this, not this...

Where's my book about beetles?

Here it is!

Thesis on Beetles

This one is too large to hunt.

This one is too small for hungry larvae.

It looks like the only beetles that are the right size for the bee to sting are the jewel beetle and the rice weevil.

Alright, incorrect facts need to be corrected. I'll write down my observations and send them to the university.

Henri researched the facts in Dufour's book which were incorrect and presented it in a paper.

Done!

Henri presented his paper entitled, *Considerations on the Behavior of Wasps and the Cause of the Long Preservation of Wasp Larvae's Beetle*.

Academic Confe

The experimental results from my observations of the wasp are as follows.

His results are the complete opposite of the results of Dufour's research!

Research on the lifestyle of insects... The research methodology is totally different from any methodology previously used. Truly remarkable!

That's great!

demic Confer

CLAP

CLAP

CLAP

98

Your paper on wasps is really impressive.

Thank you, Dr. Dufour.

I was amazed at your outstanding power of observation.

This is all due to the inspiration I received from your book. I should be the one to thank you.

Besides Dufour, the British biologist who wrote *The Origin of Species*, Charles Darwin, even highly praised Fabre's observation skills.

Jean-Henri Fabre has discovered a new path for future generations with his outstanding power of observation.

In 1856, Henri was recognized as an outstanding scholar when the Institute of France awarded his paper with the Montyon Prize.

Although Henri was now an established scholar, he was still as poor as ever.

Children continued to be born, requiring more and more money.
It became difficult to pay for expenses with just a teacher's salary.

Catch me if you can! Hahaha.

You don't think I can?

Me too, me too!

Jules, stop running around! Keep your sisters quiet. Your father's studying!

Hey, little rascals! You all seem bored. How about looking at some insects with me?

Let's see what insects are out in the yard.

Okay!

100

Life was hard but Henri spent time with his children whenever he could, and gave them lessons about nature that they could see and feel for themselves.

Alright, today we will conduct an experiment. Today's experiment...

These extra classes I have to teach make it hard to find time to do my research.

But there was never a time when things weren't hard. Actually, I've gone through tougher times than this.

I have to do this for my children.

Now let's record carefully what we did today!

Yes, sir!

Henri was the only teacher who was well-respected and didn't have a negative nickname among the students.

Good morning, Mr. Fabre!

Good morning, boys!

Mr. Fabre is my favorite teacher.

Me too! He always takes us out every Sunday to have class outside. And we can always talk to him if we have a problem!

Other teachers were jealous of Henri and ostracized him.

Henri didn't pay attention to his fellow teachers' disregard or jealousy, and did his best as a teacher.

One day, one of the school's supervisors who came to observe the school watched Henri's class with interest.

Mr. Fabre seems to be teaching his students with much care and effort. A stellar teacher like him is rare!

Mr. Fabre!

Yes, sir.

May I ask you a question? How much savings do you have?

I have not gathered much savings. The salary I get from teaching is everything I have. Why do you ask?

I read your article in *the Annals of Natural Science*.

When I look at your sense of observation, your research skills, and your vivid writing skills, you have more than enough to be a university professor.

104

Actually, I have been working on preparations to become a professor, so that I can do more research.

Unfortunately, you need an additional source of income in order to become a university professor.

Otherwise, it's difficult to obtain a position.

Really?

Henri's dream was to teach in the university in order to be fully engaged in research activity. But because he had no additional income, he could not fulfill his dream.

If I became a professor, I wouldn't have to work so hard to earn a living. Then I could do more research on insects and have more time to myself...

What are you thinking about, dear?

...

The supervisor stopped by today.

He said that in order to become a professor, I'd need another source of income. So I was trying to think of a way to make that happen.

What if you look into what's needed in this region? Something related to dye might be good.

Ah, right! The dye industry is one of the most important industries in this area!

The most important raw material used at the dye factories is madder*. The red that comes from the root of the madder is used as the raw material for dye.

*madder: A perennial vine. The leaves are eaten and the root is used in dyes. It grows to about two meters and the root is a yellowish red.

But when the madder root is boiled and crushed, red isn't the only color that is produced. Hence, good quality dye cannot be manufactured with the current technology!

If we can separate the red element in madder, the alizarin, then we as well as poor farmers can make an incredible income!

Then you'll be able to apply for a professorship again.

If this works out, I could research insects as much as I want! I'd better start working on this right now!

You can do it, dear!

Henri taught students during the day, and with any time he had left, he studied the madder root.

He succeeded in extracting the necessary substance from the madder root and presented a paper about it. He also invented and patented a way to produce madder powder.

The cotton factory was able to use Henri's method and manufacture dyed material.

Because of you, our production has increased and our lives have improved! Thank you, Mr. Fabre!

Thank you for developing a way to produce dye using madder!

However, he continued to have more children and as his family responsibilities increased, Henri's dream became more distant.

Mama, I have to pay for my school supplies.

Mama, I want to learn piano!

Let's wait a little more. When Papa gets paid, I'll give it to you.

Life hasn't gotten easier. It's actually getting harder.

Then one day, an important person paid a visit. It was Victor Duruy, the commissioner of the school where he formerly taught.

Mr. Fabre, it's been a long time.

Sir!

I remembered observing your class several years ago and decided to come pay you a visit.

Even after becoming a government minister, he did not forget about Fabre and decided to come see him.

It's an honor to have you still remember me.

The government is currently trying to reform the national education system. As minister of education, I am in charge of this.

You've become a government minister! Congratulations.

I guess this is your madder root research lab. Mr. Fabre, tell me what you need for your research. I would like to support your work.

That's alright. The equipment I have is sufficient.

The fact that you remembered me and visited are encouragement enough.

Other scientists make a big fuss to get grants for their research... But he's content researching in this shabby laboratory with worn-out lab equipment!

Mr. Fabre, I hope you will continue with your research.

Thank you, Minister Duruy.

If Fabre's madder experiment hadn't succeeded, we would've been out of work and our lives would have been much harder.

That's true. He's a great man who doesn't just think about his own profit but thinks about others first.

Half a year passed when a letter from Duruy arrived.

Honey, Minister Duruy sent us a letter.

I don't know why but he says to come to Paris.

You must accept a request from the Minister.

Some time later, Henri arrived in Paris to meet Duruy.

The reason why I insisted on you coming out here is to give you this.

What is it?

You deserve this medal, Dr. Jean -Henri Fabre.

Duruy presented Henri with the Legion d'Honneur Medal, the highest honor in France.

I can't believe I just received the highest honor in France, the Legion d'Honneur. I'd better work even harder in my research.

Henri received the medal and a monetary prize.

Your entomology research and madder experiment which has greatly benefited people more than qualifies you to earn the Legion d'Honneur medal.

However, not long afterwards, Henri's madder research became useless after a scholar in Germany developed a man-made alizarin.

Look at this! It's a man-made dye that is the same as natural dye!

And they say the manufacturing process is even easier!

Sigh, I've concentrated solely on dye research for the last few years and it's worthless now.

Henri spent the entire prize money on his research on dye and insects, but fortunately, he was able to teach at Saint Martial Convent's evening school through Duruy's appointment.

We will learn things necessary for practical life and if you apply these to farming, they will be of help to you.

Farming has become easier thanks to Mr. Fabre!

With this new agricultural method, this year's vegetable crops did very well.

People flocked to Henri's lectures.

114

He also began to work as director of the Requien Museum which was run by the convent. It was here that he met British economist John Stuart Mill. Mill had recently lost his wife and moved to Avignon to be near his wife's grave in Avignon Cemetery.

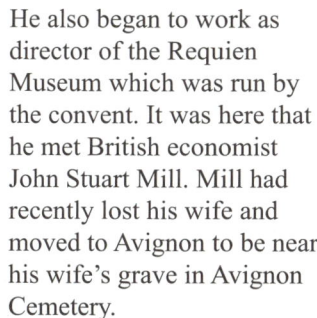

Haha, Mr. Mill! I see you've become more interested in plants these days!

My wife loved plants.

These days I've been finding pleasure in collecting plants from the field.

Because of your interest in nature, I feel like you are a kindred spirit!

Haha! That's nice of you to say that.

Days passed by peacefully but there were people who thought Henri was receiving special favors from Minister Duruy and talking about it.

He does useless research but somehow receives a lot of money!

Don't you think Fabre got the position of museum director because he had connections with Duruy?

Look at all the people who attend his low quality classes!

What?
Minister Duruy
has stepped down?

You're so close with the minister and you didn't know? That's too bad. It's going to be tough not having a minister who can look out for you.

How could this be?

Mr. Fabre, you need to vacate this house immediately!

Excuse me? How can you just tell us to vacate like this?

I've let you stay here because of the minister but now either you need to pay the higher rent or move out!

Not long after Duruy was kicked out of office, Henri was also soon kicked out of his school and his home after his coworkers slandered him.

What's happening?

It's clear that someone is maliciously slandering Minister Duruy and me!

Having poured all his money into his research, Henri had no strength as he suddenly faced this difficult situation. He decided to write a letter to his friend in England, John Stuart Mill.

Dear John,
I'm sorry to have to ask you this but I was wondering if you could loan me some money if it's possible.

It's not much but I hope it will help.

I'm so thankful for this friend.

With this, we can move tomorrow.

Alright.

In 1871, 45-year-old Henri left Avignon where he had spent about 20 years of his life, and moved to Orange.

Kids, this is our new home. Let's go in and take a look.

Yay!

07 Souvenirs Entomologiques

Jules, do you like our new home?

Yes, I really like that I can go to the woods anytime I want and look at insects.

Haha. Jules, how about going together now? We can see what insects are there.

Uh!

Jules, are you okay?

I'm okay, Papa. Just a little dizzy.

After they moved out of the city and into an isolated house in the outskirts of town, Henri occasionally went out to the woods with his son, Jules, to observe insects.

This time was financially the most difficult period for Henri. Consequently, he began to write textbooks in order to earn a living.

Papa, what are you doing up so late?

Jules, you're still awake.

This is what we're learning at school.

Right, it's a textbook.

Science class is always difficult but this book makes it look easy and fun.

If my Jules thinks that way, then I'm halfway to success.

It's going to be great to study from a book that you wrote.

Words like that from my son just lift me right up. Hahaha.

After Henri wrote up and published *Science Story*, their living situation began to improve.

I'm looking for Fabre's *Science Story*.

Me too!

Science is usually dry and boring, but this is so easy to understand and fun!

The material just sticks in my head because it's so vivid, like I'm seeing the real thing!

And there aren't any hard words in it, so it's easy to read!

From the textbook sales, Henri was able to repay the money Mill loaned him. From then on, he would teach during the day and become absorbed in writing books at night.

Papa, what book are you writing now?

It's about important harmful insects in agricultural farming. I'm going to also explain about birds, baby animals, and vertebrates that prey on these pests.

I'm also thinking about writing about the insects that I've researched up to now.

I'll help you, Papa!

Okay, but you've got to take care of your health. Got it?

Don't worry! These days, I'm eating a lot and I don't feel dizzy anymore.

Haha, good. Keep it up, Jules.

Day and night, Henri became absorbed in writing a book about insects. And when he had time, he would go around with Jules to find specimens of insects and plants.

Papa, there's a wasp and a similar insect here!

Let's see.

You've discovered a new kind of bee!

Henri's son Jules was his biggest helper as he wrote *Souvenirs Entomologiques*.

I want to help you in your entomology research!

Whether you help or not, you're my best cheerleader.

Henri really loved his son, Jules, who enjoyed collecting insects. But there were many days when Jules was ill because of his weak health.

Do you think we'll find a new bee tomorrow, too? Papa, I really like collecting bugs. Let's go tomorrow, too.

Of course, but your health is first priority. I think you'd better rest tomorrow.

Then one day, Henri went to look for his son to go insect hunting together.

Jules!

Jules, get up!

It's my fault. He hasn't been well, and I've been taking him out too much.

It's not your fault. Jules will regain his consciousness any minute.

I want to go out with you to find some insects, Papa. I'm sorry I can't get up right now.

I'm going to hurry and finish the insect book for you. Get better so we can go collect insects again, okay?

Yes, Papa...

However, Henri was not able to go collecting insects with Jules again. Having always been ill his whole life, Jules passed away at the age of 16 on September 14, 1877.

In order to cope with the loss of his son, Henri delved deeper into his entomology research.

Another incorrect assertion.

I made it difficult for the dung beetle to roll the ball of dung by keeping it in place with some needles and making a pit so that the ball would fall into the trap. But in no circumstance did the beetle enlist the help of another beetle!

What looked like two beetles rolling a ball together was actually beetles that were fighting to take possession of the ball.

This was another assertion that was not based on proper observation!

And finally in 1879, the year Henri turned 56 years old, the first volume of *Souvenirs Entomologiques* was published. He named three of the bees, which his son Jules had discovered (wasp, digger wasp, and another kind of digger wasp), after his son.

Jules, do you remember the insects you discovered?

I named them after you.

My dear son, Jules, you were the reason I started writing this book, and I'm going to continue this work for your sake. You can watch me from up above. I love you, Jules.

It's so interesting! I've never seen a book so exciting!

My goodness! This book has so much detailed information about insects!

Mama, I wanna see, too!

Not only was Henri's *Souvenirs Entomologiques* well received as a children's educational book, but it was highly praised among scholars as well. This book read like a movie vividly portraying Fabre's motivation for observing insects, the process of observation, the joy, and the results.

One cannot help but be amazed at the plethora of new discoveries.

It's like an insect revolution.

Henri had some free time, for once in a long time.

CHIRP CHIRP CHIRP CHIRP CHIRP

Hmm? Even though I'm standing right next to it, it's not flying away.

This summer is undoubtedly a big year for cicadas!

CLAP CLAP

It's not flying away even when I clap.

But even during his free time, Henri was always experimenting.

Aha! Cicadas have good eyesight, but they have poor hearing!

I have to find out! I have to see whether cicadas can hear or not!

Henri immediately went to city hall to borrow a cannon that was used for festivals and brought it to his yard.

What's he going to do with that cannon?

CHIRP
CHIRP
CHIRP

I tell you, Fabre is a strange man. Does he need it for his insect research?

BOOM

Ah, my eardrums!

Whoa!

Are their ears really bad?

CHIRP CHIRP

CHIRP
CHIRP

Cicadas could discern other cicadas' cries but they could not hear anything else. However this fact was discovered later, after Henri had passed away.

I'm certain that cicadas have poor hearing. Otherwise, they wouldn't have been able to stay still and continue making their cries if they had heard the sound of the booming cannon.

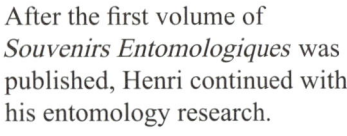
After the first volume of *Souvenirs Entomologiques* was published, Henri continued with his entomology research.

THWACK
THWACK

...

Wh-what? The owner is ruthlessly chopping down that sycamore tree!

THWACK
THWACK

Oh dear, he's chopped down all the branches.

It's going to be difficult to continue my cicada research.

I can't stand the suffocation of the city. I want to live in a place where we can experience nature.

Let's do that, dear.

Henri was finally able to purchase a house with the earnings he made from his books.

Our very own home. This is exactly the kind of home I've wanted!

You've worked hard, honey.

I've always wanted to live in a house like this. The land is rough but it's the best place for thistles and insects.

Although he quit teaching at the school, he was able to make a comfortable living publishing books.

I've got to work on writing more of *Souvenirs Entomologiques* again.

Henri felt much freedom to do research at his new home in Ales.

Out of the research lab and in the middle of nature! No longer the work of keeping insects trapped and cutting them to pieces, but observing them as they go about their normal lives!

Let's not study death but life!

It was easy to find the home of a pedicornis bee in the gravel near his house.

Pedicornis bees make their home by mixing their venom with the sand particles!

He also observed the colorful honey bee.

This honey bee makes itself seen with its stripes.

It's the digger wasp and the grasshopper. It looks like the wasp is dragging the grasshopper into the sand pit that it dug.

For several days, Henri cleared the field of pebbles and planted tree saplings.

There.

How will it look when all these trees have fully grown?

Not long afterwards, the trees became full and each plant grew so that it became a haven for insects and birds.

Haha! This place should be a good place to find insects without having to go far out.

All the hard work was worth it. It looks beautiful!

It's like the garden of Eden itself. Hahaha.

Henri published the second volume of *Souvenirs Entomologiques* and three years later in 1885, his wife passed away when he was 62. Two years later, Henri remarried and beginning with his son Paul, had three more children. Paul, who learned photography, took about 200 pictures of insects under his father's guidance, which were then used in his father's book.

The more I take pictures of insects, the more interesting they become. What do you think, Father?

They turned out well, Paul.

In 1882, the second volume of *Souvenirs Entomologiques* was published and four years later, the third volume came out.

In 1907, the final volume of *Souvenirs Entomologiques,* Volume 10, marked 28 years since the publication of the first volume.

Finally, the last volume is complete!

However the response towards this volume was not very good and not many were sold.

Souvenirs Entomologiques? What's this?

Let's go. You don't have time to read that.

The content of textbooks has long since been revised.

This is an outdated book.

Because the textbooks had been revised and the content of his book didn't match them, his income decreased and their finances became tight again.

I'm worried because the books are not selling very well, Father.

You were a big help in writing the books. I'm sorry you're not benefiting much from your hard work.

Then one day, Frederic Mistral, a famous French poet, paid Henri a visit.

I respect your work so I came to pay you a visit.

Welcome, Mr. Mistral.

This great entomologist is living such a shabby life!

I'm sorry we don't have much to serve you.

How is it that you are living such a difficult life?

It's not a difficult life to be enjoying nature. I am the happiest that I have been my entire life.

I can see insects whenever I want right now.

Henri recollected the times when he roamed around freely to observe insects on his grandfather's farm.

When I was young, my grandfather would tell me the names of each insect and how each one lived in detail.

Afterwards, I began to develop a passion for entomology and *Souvenirs Entomologiques* was born.

The knowledge I have gained from my research on everything from the dung beetle to the wasp to the madder has been more than enough to bring me happiness in my life. And it will continue to bring me happiness.

I have to let more people know about this great man's *Souvenirs Entomologiques*, which captures his spirit!

Let's give another chance for people to be exposed to *Souvenirs Entomologiques*.

What do you mean?

Let's hold an anniversary event for the publication of your books!

In that way, your books will be publicized to the world again!

On April 3, 1910, there was a publication anniversary event for 87-year-old Henri. This day was declared as Fabre Day, many people came to congratulate him, and *Souvenirs Entomologiques* was reintroduced to the world.

Congratulations, sir!

You are truly amazing to have written such a book!

Souvenirs Entomologiques is the best!

And in 1913, the final illustrated edition of *Souvenirs Entomologiques*, which included the 200 photographs taken by his son, Paul, was published.

Jean-Henri Fabre, who spent his whole life searching for truth through research, spent his last moments enjoying the warm sun coming through the window on October 11, 1915. Then he became one with the nature he loved.

"When I daydream, I wish, for just a few minutes, I could think with the brain of our dog. I have also wished to see the world through the eyes of a fly. How different the things of this world would look!"

From Critical Biography of Fabre

Word Search

● Find the words which are hidden horizontally, vertically and diagonally.

```
G M Z G Q M Z L I C E N S E M Z G Q M T
W S X N V E N T I O N H W W N A H W N O
E B Q J A B Q J E T B A R B A R I O B M
R V C M E T H O D O L O G Y V C K N O M
E C W U R S E N T C D L T T C D U P R E
V X E Q Y X E O L X E Q Y Y Y X E N O I M
E Z V W U D V W C E V W T U Z V J R N W
A N A E I N E E I A C E E I A R A T G I
L S I R O S A C O S T T C O S G S U S T
P D C A P D H T O D H E U P D H T N D A
A F A Y H F U Y U T U Y V R F U Y I F D
S G S U S T I N C R I G E I E G U T G R
D S S I D H M I D H E I R D H O I Y H A
F A A B S O R A F J T J F F J T J F J W
G L N B G K R E R E P I E N T S B G K C
H A A N H L E N H E E N H H L E N H L E
J R T M J Q T A U O S T R A C I Z E B T
L Y E Q L W Y Q L W Y Q L L W Y Q L U Y
Z W K F Z W K F Z W K F Z Z S U F T Y R
X E M E X J R I N C I P A L E M U X N M
C R Q T C R Q C P I N F O R M A T I O N
```

| nature | salary | license | methodology |
| lecture | ostracize | boring | information |

Vocabulary

● Match each word to the correct meaning.

1. farmer   • 곤충

2. count on   • 연구하다

3. investigate   • 농부

4. entomologist   • 믿다

5. insect   • 곤충학자

6. contrary to ~   • 자유

7. objective   • 묘사하다

8. biologist   • 공상에 잠기다

9. responsibility   • ～와는 반대로

10. portray   • 생물학자

11. freedom   • 목적, 목표

12. daydream   • 책임

Lesson 3

Guess What?

● Guess what she said in the blank.

However, the Fabre family's financial situation continued to grow worse. They had moved to Montpellier, but their business did not do well there, either. In the end, they had to separate from each other and live in different places.

Every time we've started a new business, it hasn't done well so we've accumulated a lot of debt.

So we decided that your father and I will go to a bigger city to earn money.

And Frederic will stay at a relative's house.

I'm fifteen now. Don't worry, Father.

Father, Mother, take good care of yourselves! Frederic, see you again soon!

Henri!

Take care, Henri!

CLOP CLOP

Six Groups of Animals

Mammals

koala (코알라)

There are about 5,000 species of living mammals in the world. Mammals have fur or hair. They are warm-blooded and feed their babies milk from their own bodies.

Most mammals give birth to live young, but a few primitive mammals like the duck-billed platypus lay eggs.

Different types of mammals include vegetation eating herbivores such as cows, horses, pandas; meat eating carnivores such as whales, dolphins, dogs, lions, tigers; omnivores which eat both plants and meat such as people, bears; while insectivores include such animals as aardvarks, anteaters, pangolins which eat only insects.

The fastest mammal is the cheetah, the slowest mammal is the sloth. The biggest mammal, actually the biggest of all animals on Earth is the blue whale.

Birds

robin (울새)

Birds are warm-blooded vertebrate animals that have wings and feathers. Most birds can fly but not all flying animals are birds. Bats can fly, but they are mammals. And not all birds can fly. Penguins can't fly but can swim. Ostriches can't fly but can run very fast.

Flying birds have strong, hollow bones which are very light and powerful flight muscles.

Male birds are usually more brightly colored than females in order to attract females for mating. The females usually have less colored feathers to camouflage her when she cares for her eggs and young.

Many birds migrate avoiding the cold weather of winter.

Amphibians

tree frog (청개구리)

Amphibians are born in the water and can live in the water by breathing with gills. As they grow, they breathe air with lungs and live on the land.

Amphibians are vertebrates and hatches from eggs. Amphibians include frogs, toads, salamanders and newts.

Frogs eat insects, catching them with their long sticky tongues. Most frogs have teeth in the upper jaws but toads don't have any teeth.

Amphibians are cold-blooded, so their body temperature changes with their environment. That's why frogs usually hibernate through the cold winter.

Frogs spend their lives near water to lay their eggs in the water. When they hatch from eggs into tadpoles, they breathe with gills and have a tail. As they grow they lose their tail and develop lungs for breathing. Other amphibians also have similar life cycles.

Reptiles

green snake (청사)

Reptiles are vertebrates with scales that can breathe air with their lungs. They usually lay eggs. Since they are cold-blooded, they use the sunlight and their surroundings to heat their bodies. Many of them hibernate during the winter, and some reptiles are poisonous. Typical reptiles are snakes, crocodiles, lizards, and turtles.

The biggest reptile is the estuarine crocodile which is over 7 m. The smallest reptile is the British Virgin Islands gecko which is only 18 mm. The biggest snake is the anaconda of South America. The biggest lizard is the Komodo dragon which is up to 3 m long. The biggest turtle is the leatherback turtle growing up to 2.5 m.

Fish

tropical fish (열대어)

Fish are cold-blooded vertebrate animals that live in water. Some fish live in fresh water and some live in salty ocean water. Fish are covered with scales and have streamlined muscular bodies.

Whales look like a fish and live in the ocean. But they are considered mammals rather than fish as they breathe through their lungs, forcing them to come up to the surface for air. Fish breathe with gills and get their oxygen from the water.

Most fish have bony skeletons, but some such as sharks and rays have only cartilage.

Insect

bee (벌)

Insects are small animals that have three body parts. The three body parts are the head, the thorax, and the abdomen. The legs and wings are attached to the thorax.

Insects breathe through holes called spiracles.

And all insects have a hard exoskeleton, compound eyes, and two antennae. All insects hatch from eggs.

Many insects can fly. Flying insects such as butterflies, moths, dragonflies, flies, and mosquitos have one or two pairs of wings.

An insect's life cycle has unique stages, and is called metamorphosis. For example, an ant lays eggs, and the eggs hatch into larvae. When larva grow big enough, they spin a cocoon around themselves to become pupa. In the cocoon they transform and emerge as an adult, such as when a caterpillar becomes a butterfly.

There are about a million different kinds of insects on Earth and many are not yet discovered.

1823년	12월 22일, 프랑스 남부 생 레옹의 작은 마을에서 태어납니다.
1830년 7세	초등학교에 입학합니다.
1838년 15세	가정 형편이 어려워 가족들이 흩어져 살게 됩니다.
1839년 16세	아비뇽 사범학교에 입학합니다.
1842년 19세	카르팡트라스 학교의 초등 교사로 부임합니다.
1844년 21세	같은 학교 선생님인 마리 비야르와 결혼합니다.
1848년 25세	몽펠리에 대학에서 수학과 물리학 학사 자격을 얻습니다.
1849년 26세	코르시카의 아작시오 중학교의 물리 교사가 됩니다.
1853년 30세	열병에 걸려 치료를 위해 도시로 돌아옵니다. 아비뇽 고등학교 교사로 부임합니다.
1855년 32세	논문 「노래기벌의 습성과 그 애벌레의 먹이로 이용되는 딱정벌레류의 장기간 보존 원인에 대한 고찰」을 발표합니다.

1856년 33세	꼭두서니 뿌리로부터 염료인 알리자린을 뽑아내는 연구를 시작합니다.
1861년 38세	아비뇽에 있는 르키앙 박물관장에 임명됩니다. 아들 쥘이 태어납니다.
1865년 42세	파스퇴르가 누에 전염병을 연구하기 위해 아비뇽을 방문합니다.
1868년 45세	꼭두서니 연구에 대한 공로를 인정받아 레종 도뇌르 훈장을 받습니다.
1871년 48세	어린이를 위한 과학 이야기를 쓰기 시작합니다.
1877년 54세	9월 14일, 아들 쥘이 사망합니다. 파브르는 쥘이 발견한 곤충들 중에서 세 가지에 쥘의 이름을 붙여 줍니다.
1878년 55세	알마스로 이사합니다.
1879년 56세	『곤충기』 1권을 펴냅니다.
1907년 84세	『곤충기』 10권을 펴냅니다.
1910년 87세	4월 3일, 파브르의 날이 선포됩니다.
1915년 92세	10월 11일, 세상을 떠납니다.

who? 01	Barack Obama	979-11-5639-023-7
who? 02	Charles Darwin	979-11-5639-024-4
who? 03	Bill Gates	979-11-5639-025-1
who? 04	Hillary Clinton	979-11-5639-026-8
who? 05	Stephen Hawking	979-11-5639-027-5
who? 06	Oprah Winfrey	979-11-5639-028-2
who? 07	Steven Spielberg	979-11-5639-029-9
who? 08	Thomas Edison	979-11-5639-030-5
who? 09	Abraham Lincoln	979-11-5639-031-2
who? 10	Martin Luther King, Jr.	979-11-5639-032-9
who? 11	Louis Braille	979-11-5639-033-6
who? 12	Albert Einstein	979-11-5639-034-3
who? 13	Jane Goodall	979-11-5639-035-0
who? 14	Walt Disney	979-11-5639-036-7
who? 15	Winston Churchill	979-11-5639-037-4
who? 16	Warren Buffett	979-11-5639-008-4
who? 17	Nelson Mandela	979-11-5639-009-1
who? 18	Steve Jobs	979-11-5639-010-7
who? 19	J. K. Rowling	979-11-5639-011-4
who? 20	Jean-Henri Fabre	979-11-5639-012-1
who? 21	Vincent van Gogh	979-11-5639-013-8
who? 22	Marie Curie	979-11-5639-014-5
who? 23	Henry David Thoreau	979-11-5639-015-2
who? 24	Andrew Carnegie	979-11-5639-016-9
who? 25	Coco Chanel	979-11-5639-017-6
who? 26	Charlie Chaplin	979-11-5639-018-3
who? 27	Ho Chi Minh	979-11-5639-019-0
who? 28	Ludwig van Beethoven	979-11-5639-020-6
who? 29	Mao Zedong	979-11-5639-021-3
who? 30	Kim Dae-jung	979-11-5639-022-0